Mystery of the Ancient Pueblo

by Kathy Furgang

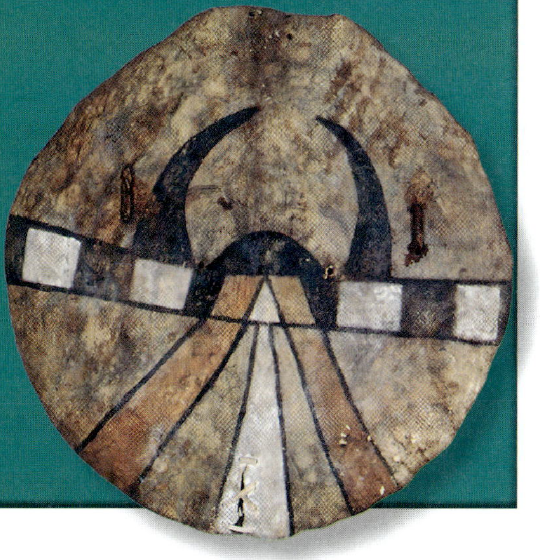

Scott Foresman
is an imprint of

PEARSON

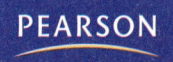

Glenview, Illinois • Boston, Massachusetts • Chandler, Arizona •
Upper Saddle River, New Jersey

Illustrations
23 George Hamblin.

Photographs

Every effort has been made to secure permission and provide appropriate credit for photographic material. The publisher deeply regrets any omission and pledges to correct errors called to its attention in subsequent editions.

Unless otherwise acknowledged, all photographs are the property of Pearson Education, Inc.

Photo locators denoted as follows: Top (T), Center (C), Bottom (B), Left (L), Right (R), Background (Bkgd)

Opener National Geographic/Corbis; **1** Lowe Art Museum/SuperStock; **4** Carl Iwasaki/Time Life Pictures/Getty Images; **5** The Cliff Dweller by John Norton/Logan Museum of Anthropology and Wright Museum of Art; **6** (BR) Bill Hatcher/National Geographic Image Collection, (BL) Russ Bishop/PhotoLibrary Group, Inc.; **7** ©Judith Miller/Domas & Gray Gallery/©DK Images; **9** Kevin Fleming/Corbis; **11** ©AP Images; **12** (BL) ©Dietrich Rose/Getty Images; **13** Edward S. Curtis/Corbis; **15** Bettmann/Corbis; **16** (TL) Lowe Art Museum/SuperStock; **17** National Geographic/Getty Images; **18** National Geographic/Corbis; **21** Gail Mooney/Corbis; **22** Mark Rykoff/Corbis.

ISBN 13: 978-0-328-52564-5
ISBN 10:   0-328-52564-2

Copyright © Pearson Education, Inc. or its affiliate(s). All Rights Reserved.
Printed in the United States of America. This publication is protected by copyright and permission should be obtained from the publisher prior to any prohibited reproduction, storage in a retrieval system, or transmission in any form or by any means, electronic, mechanical, photocopying, recording, or otherwise. For information regarding permission(s), write to: Pearson School Rights and Permissions, One Lake Street, Upper Saddle River, New Jersey 07458.

Pearson and Scott Foresman are trademarks, in the U.S. and/or other countries, of Pearson Education, Inc. or its affiliate(s).

2 3 4 5 6 7 8 9 10 V0N4 13 12 11 10

Table of Contents

Chapter 1 4
Looking into the Past

Chapter 2 6
Life of the Ancient Pueblo

Chapter 3 10
Why Did the Ancient Pueblo Leave?

Now Try This 22

Chapter 1 Looking into the Past

How can we learn about cultures that lived before there were written records? What can these people teach us about ourselves? When we look into our past, we must act like detectives trying to solve a mystery.

One of the most interesting **ancient** civilizations that scientists have uncovered in the Americas dates back to about 1200 BCE. This civilization is the Ancient Pueblo, sometimes known as Ancestral Puebloans or the Anasazi. These ancestors of today's Pueblo lived in what is today the southwestern United States, especially around the area now known as the Four Corners—the place where Utah, Colorado, New Mexico, and Arizona meet.

This ancient people first lived on the tops of mesas, small plateaus with dramatically steep sides and relatively flat tops. Around 1200 CE the Ancient Pueblo moved to more hidden homes in canyon walls. Finally, they abandoned the area altogether. Where did these people go? Why did they leave? **Archaeologists** and other scientists are looking for the answers to these questions. The more we learn about how the Ancient Pueblo lived, the more we may learn about what made them leave their homes.

An early monument at the Four Corners—the spot where four southwestern states meet—in 1949

An Ancient Pueblo cliff dwelling

When we learn about an ancient civilization, we are really learning about ourselves too. Knowing what might have made the Ancient Pueblo disappear may make us aware of dangers that our own society may face.

The Ancient Pueblo have left us a lot of **evidence** of their lifestyle. Archaeologists have found their homes, **artifacts**, and even their remains. This gives us clues to how they lived and how they may have died.

Why did the Ancient Pueblo once live on the tops of mesas in the wide open, and then suddenly begin living in more hidden homes cut out of canyon walls? What changed in their lives that made them decide to do this? Even scientists who hold evidence in their hands cannot truly know what an ancient civilization went through.

Chapter 2 Life of the Ancient Pueblo

The Ancient Pueblo were great architects. Today their stunning cliff dwellings draw thousands of visitors every year to Mesa Verde National Park in Colorado. The area was preserved as a national park so that these lands would remain untouched and so that people could learn about this ancient culture.

The cliff dwellings are amazing feats of architecture, especially considering that the Ancient Pueblo had only stone tools. Using these tools, they broke up boulders and moved them to form rooms in the cliffside. Boulders that were too big or hard to break up were sometimes left in place and made part of the structure. The Ancient Pueblo also used adobe, a mixture of clay and straw, as mortar and plaster to strengthen and smooth out walls and window openings.

The builders added upper floors to their homes by laying large beams across boulders. Smaller beams running crosswise to the larger beams created a surface strong enough to build on.

Some of the buildings had large circular rooms called **kivas**. These were used for religious ceremonies and perhaps as meeting places or family spaces.

The Ancient Pueblo were not only skilled builders, they were talented **artisans**. They made clay pottery that featured intricate designs colored with natural dyes. The Ancient Pueblo cooked, served, and gathered food and water in clay pots. They also used the pots in ceremonial and burial practices. The pots were part of everyday life, so archaeologists rarely find a perfectly preserved pot. Many of them are faded, broken, or chipped.

Making clay pots involves sculpting and firing. It is likely that the Ancient Pueblo first made woven baskets, then lined them with clay. When placed on a fire, the baskets would have burned away, leaving the clay in the form of a pot. This is one of the earliest firing methods, and it may have been used by many Native American groups.

The Ancient Pueblo lived in the Four Corners area for hundreds of years. Then, over the span of about a generation, large groups of Ancient Pueblo left their cliff dwellings behind. Archaeologists have found no evidence at all of the Ancient Pueblo in the Four Corners area after about 1300 CE. What happened to this impressive culture? Why would they abandon their homes?

Historians think that they know where these people went: they moved to the area that is now New Mexico and Arizona. But why did they move there? It has been a question and a mystery for several decades. There are many **theories**, but no one knows for sure what really happened.

When studying a time before there were written records, we can only rely on the evidence we gather from the artifacts and other remains of a culture. We are not likely to prove that any one theory is true, but, over time, some theories may be disproved—narrowing down our ideas and giving us a better look into the past.

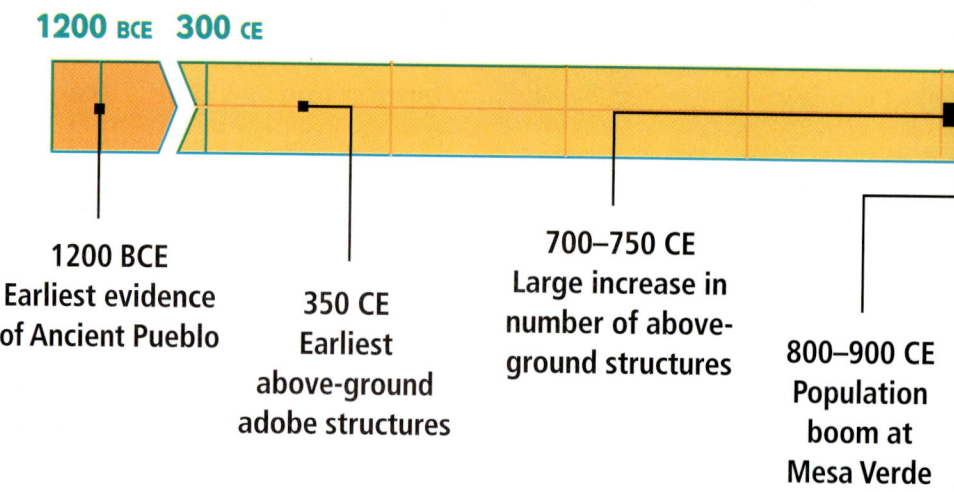

1200 BCE 300 CE

1200 BCE
Earliest evidence of Ancient Pueblo

350 CE
Earliest above-ground adobe structures

700–750 CE
Large increase in number of above-ground structures

800–900 CE
Population boom at Mesa Verde

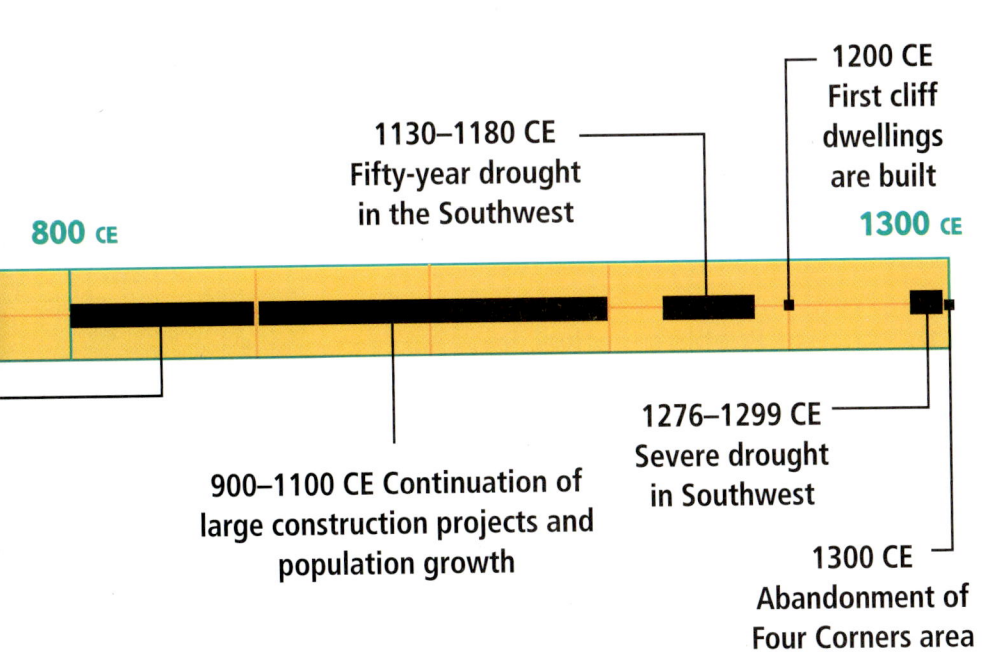

- 800 CE
- 900–1100 CE Continuation of large construction projects and population growth
- 1130–1180 CE Fifty-year drought in the Southwest
- 1200 CE First cliff dwellings are built
- 1276–1299 CE Severe drought in Southwest
- 1300 CE Abandonment of Four Corners area
- 1300 CE

9

Chapter 3 Why Did the Ancient Pueblo Leave?

If you were an archaeologist trying to solve the mystery of an ancient culture, where would you start? Artifacts give us clues to the past, and so do scientific methods. Scientists use these methods to answer specific questions. Are there mass graves in these ancient lands? Is there evidence of war or other violence? Is there scientific data that proves a severe drought occurred? The answers to these questions can help give people of our own time a glimpse into this unknown world.

Paleontologists, people who study fossils of ancient plants and animals, have a handful of theories about why the Ancient Pueblo left the area of the Four Corners and moved deeper into the areas that are now Arizona and New Mexico. Archaeologists too, after sifting through the evidence, have recently proposed new theories about the Ancient Pueblo's motives for leaving. Each theory has its merits; each has its discrepancies. Read each theory, and then decide which one you believe!

Was there a drought?

One of the most popular theories about why the Ancient Pueblo left their homes suggests that a severe, long-lasting drought made the area uninhabitable. Scientists have confirmed that there was a long period with very little rain around the time the Ancient Pueblo began moving away.

Scientists learned of the drought by looking at tree trunks! If you cut the trunk of a tree, you will find a pattern of rings inside that tells a story. As a tree grows, the trunk gets thicker so it can support its added height and weight. Every year, a tree grows another ring. In times of plentiful rainfall, the tree grows quickly, so its rings are farther apart. During very dry times, the tree gets less water to grow, so the rings are closer together.

After examining trees in the area where the Ancient Pueblo lived, scientists were able to pinpoint a time, from 1274 to 1299, when the tree rings were close together. This signals that it was a time of drought, a time when there would have been less for people to eat because their crops did not get enough water to grow.

If the Ancient Pueblo experienced a prolonged drought around this time, it would explain why they moved away over a span of years instead of all at once. A drought of twenty-five years would have allowed them to notice its long-term effects. Families would have had less and less food as the years went on. They might have finally decided that it was time to leave and look for a better place to live.

At the start of the 1900s, the Pueblo still used the methods of their ancestors to collect water.

Not everyone is satisfied with this theory, however. Some people think that the drought would not have been enough reason for the Ancient Pueblo to leave. By examining even older trees, scientists found that these people had lived in the area through even worse droughts than the one in the late 1200s. Could another problem have combined with the drought to make life unbearable?

Did they run out of resources?

Over the course of the 1200s, the Ancient Pueblo population grew. People moved from the mesas to cliff dwellings, where they built bigger and bigger homes. The "cliff palace" at Mesa Verde is a good example of a large Ancient Pueblo structure that housed many people. Could an increase in population have caused a scarcity of resources? Scientists think it is possible.

In the early settlements of the Ancient Pueblo, paleontologists have found the bones of large animals such as deer and elk. This suggests that these animals roamed the area during that time and were hunted for food. These animals could have provided food for large numbers of people.

Many of the later communities did not leave evidence of these large animals. Only the remains of rabbits and other small animals have been found near these settlements. This suggests to scientists that food supplies were running out.

With fewer resources in the area, people would have had less reason to live there. The Ancient Pueblo may have thought this was a good reason to move on. The fact that they left many of their dwellings intact may indicate that they intended to return to these homes eventually. Could they have left to hunt in other areas, hoping to bring food back home to their cliff dwellings?

Unlike her ancestors, this Pueblo woman had enough resources to feed her family.

One important resource in an area is water. The Ancient Pueblo built their homes in areas near water sources such as springs, rivers, and streams. If the theory is correct that a severe drought hit the area, water would be another resource that was spread thinly. Just when a larger population created a need for extra resources, drought made these resources difficult to find.

Santa Ana Pueblo Shield

Were there threats from other people?

The Ancient Pueblo are known by many people as the Anasazi. But today's Pueblo peoples would prefer that the term not be used to describe their ancestors. Why is that? The answer may be a clue to our mystery. In the Navajo language, the word *anasazi* means "ancient enemy" or "enemy of our people."

That is a big clue to historians about the relationship between the Navajo and the Ancient Pueblo. Did the two peoples battle each other during the 1200s? Perhaps the Ancient Pueblo left out of fear of their enemies.

One area where the Ancient Pueblo built their rock dwellings is called Canyon de Chelly (pronounced "duh SHAY"). It is within Navajo territory, and Navajo still live in the area today. However, the Navajo did not come to this area until years after the Pueblo had abandoned it.

So who were the Ancient Pueblo afraid of, if anyone? Their homes were not easily accessible to outsiders. They used ladders to get into their homes, and the ladders could easily be raised if the people were under attack. The rock homes provided good shelter against attack as well. Is

Pueblo Bonito, an Ancient Pueblo ruin, Chaco Canyon, New Mexico

this what the Ancient Pueblo had in mind when they built their structures? Were they hiding in the canyon from an outside enemy?

There is no evidence that major wars took place on these Ancient Pueblo grounds. However, scientists have found human remains that show evidence of violent death. Some suggest that while the drought may not have forced a mass migration, it may have entailed new forms of land use that sparked conflicts among the population groups. The thirteenth century may have been a time of mutual raiding.

But even if the Ancient Pueblo were enemies of the Navajo, would that have been enough to make the Ancient Pueblo leave their homes and seek out a new land? Historians are still trying to answer that question.

Was there an epidemic?

What other theories could explain the disappearance of this culture—apart from drought, overpopulation, overuse of resources, or threat from enemies? An epidemic is another possibility that scientists have considered.

Archaeologists have found no sign of large numbers of people dying at one time, as would be the case if an epidemic had spread through the area. Possibly, though, people could see that an epidemic was developing. Would such a threat be enough to make them leave the area? If so, that would explain the lack of evidence of large-scale deaths.

Which theory correctly explains the mystery of the Ancient Pueblo and their departure from the Four Corners area? No one knows for sure, but it probably involves a combination of two or more of these theories.

Did they leave for a new religion?

There are some archaeologists who argue that the Anasazi people were drawn from their home by a promising new religion. Religious symbols on rocks and pottery and new architecture that included secret rooms for religious rituals are representative of a different faith—a Kachina-like religion that was emerging among neighbors to the south. Perhaps the Anasazi people left to join this new, vibrant religion.

The evidence for this theory is not strong, but archaeologists do know that the Anasazi people did not build traditional Anasazi ceremonial structures in their new home. Skeptics don't believe this evidence is proof enough: Why would the Anasazi people need to leave their homes to practice their new religion?

It is unclear whether the Ancient Pueblo meant to move away from their homes for good or whether they hoped to come back someday. Scientists and historians have already learned a lot about this ancient culture just by looking at physical evidence. If the Ancient Pueblo had written records, they might have told a very different story, or they might have confirmed one of the theories that scientists and historians have proposed.

Learning about the past helps us learn about our own culture. Some of the reasons proposed for the disappearance of the Ancient Pueblo sound similar to challenges we face today. Overpopulation and overuse of natural resources is a problem in our own society. We, too, face threat from outside cultures as well as dangers from drought and other climate problems. Epidemics have been a lurking menace ever since civilization began.

Perhaps one day we will learn more about the Ancient Pueblo. And perhaps one day people will look back on our own culture and understand how we lived and what was important to us.

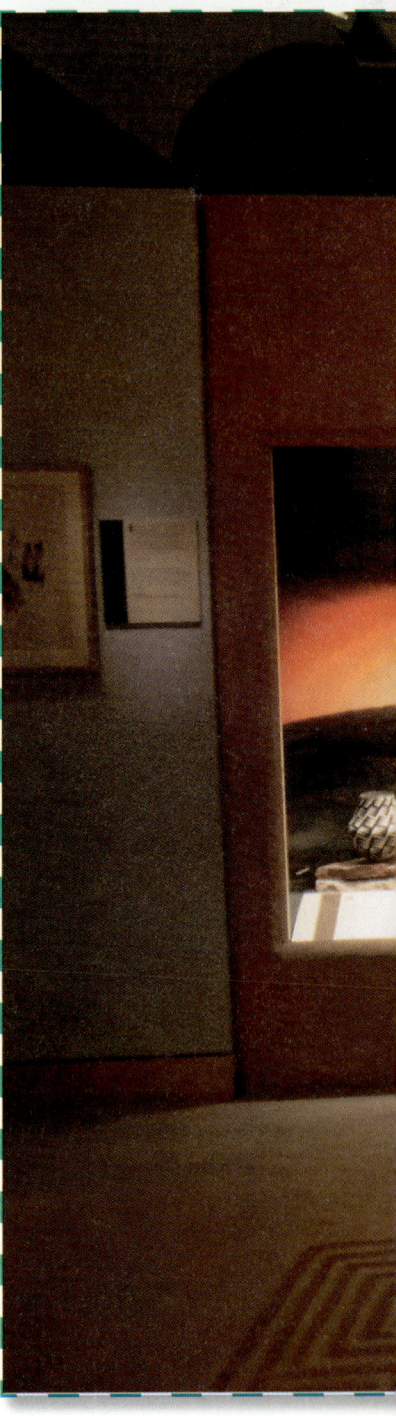

A pueblo-style exhibit in a gallery at the National Museum of the American Indian in New York City

Now Try This

Be a Detective

A lack of natural resources was one of the theories to explain why the Ancient Pueblo left their homes in the cliff dwellings near today's Four Corners area of the Southwest.

Find out about the natural resources of this area of the country. You can start with the ones mentioned in the book—water, deer, and elk. Then find out about other resources in the area.

Draw a map of the Four Corners area, and indicate on the map where these resources come from and what they are used for. Present your map to the class.